A taste of M.....y

Malagasy proverbs collected and
curated by John Stewart

Table of Contents

What makes a proverb a proverb?

There isn't just one definition for "proverb."

Defining proverbs and interpreting their meanings are daunting tasks, and academics have dedicated their careers to describing their properties. Lord John Russell remarked that proverbs could be considered as the "wit of one and the wisdom of many;" Wolfgang Mieder gave a more definitive description, characterizing the proverb as a "short, well-known sentence that conveys wisdom, truth, morals and traditional views in a metaphorical and memorizable form."

Good enough for me. I've lived and worked on every continent except Antarctica and studied more than 30 languages over the past three decades; collecting proverbs was a means of expanding my vocabulary and understanding of a culture. While I still enjoy the vocabularic souvenirs embedded in proverbs, it became more important to glean wisdom from their meaning to apply to real life. And, in promoting proverbs through my works, I've found purpose in their collection, curation and preservation for future generations.

What our sayings say about us

Proverbs encapsulate what a society perceives as wisdom, and can offer practical advice to navigate life's complexities, even at the risk of oversimplifying or misapplying their meanings. Independent of their utility, however, proverbs are important clues to how people in the past made sense of the world around them, and point to the values and beliefs of a culture.

Maybe most importantly, proverbs touch on themes like love, grief, fear, ambition and hope, illustrating the commonalities that exist across different cultures and time periods and pointing to a universal human experience that underpins every society - we may feel alone, but we are never as alone as we think we are.

This book is a companion for the slightly more sophisticated traveler, a cornucopia of vocabulary for the language learner and a guide for knowledge seekers. It can hitch a ride in a backpack or collect dust on a coffee table; its pages are destined to be dogeared and occasionally visited by the curious, the restless and those seeking their next step on their personal path of enlightenment. I know I am.

Malagasy's place in the world

More than 25 million people speak the Austronesian language Malagasy, and it's the official language of Madagascar. There are also Malagasy-speaking communities outside of Madagascar, including the neighboring islands in the Indian Ocean, such as the Comoros, Réunion, and Mauritius, as well as communities in Europe and North America.

Madagascar's strategic location off the southeastern coast of Africa created trade routes between Asia, Europe, the Middle East and other parts of Africa that turned it into the cultural crossroads that it is today. With trade routes came the Southeast Asian, Bantu, Arabic and European language influences that enriched Malagasy's lexicon and proverbs.

Today, Malagasy is used less as a language of trade, but it's still the primary language of education and an important language of expression that helps preserve the island's unique blend of cultural influences captured in its fine arts, values and traditional practices. Madagascar's relevance as a modern trade hub also helps to ensure that Malagasy will continue to contribute to the global tapestry of languages and cultures.

"Zaza tsy mba maintsy miankina fa vitsy ny mahay."

"Children do not have to agree, but they have to learn from each other."

- *Joseph Ravoahangy Andrianavalona (1913-1975)*

Malagasy proverbs

Akoho maniraka atody vorona tsy mahavita mivandravandra.

A chicken that hatches a crocodile's eggs is looking for trouble.

Getting involved in dangerous or risky situations can lead to problems.

Aoka ho vy ny fiarahamoninao; raha mitrongy dia azo hampirongatra.

May your friendship be like iron: when it breaks, you can weld the pieces back together.

Strong and resilient relationships can be repaired even if they face challenges.

Aza adino ny vokatra raisina avy

amin'ny faritra.

Do not forget the harvest from the fields.

Always remember and appreciate your roots and where you come from.

Aza atao ny sakafo, fa ny jamba.

Do not make a meal of the yam, but the peel.

Focus on the essential and important aspects of life, not superficial or trivial matters.

Aza ho vato ny fiarahamoninao; raha mitrongy dia tsy azo hampirongatra.

May your friendship not be like a stone: if it breaks, you cannot put the pieces together.

Value and nurture your friendships, as repairing broken relationships can be difficult.

Aza manao sakoriana, na tia, na tsy tia.

Do not act like a gecko, whether you like it or not.

Be true to yourself and your feelings, rather than changing your behavior to please others.

Aza manao toy ny adala, tsy mba misy fahendrena.

Do not be like the fool, there is no wisdom.

Be wise and thoughtful in your actions, rather than making foolish decisions.

Aza manao toy ny akoho maty, tsy mba misy fahendrena.

Do not be like the dead chicken, there is no wisdom.

Be wise and thoughtful in your actions, rather than impulsive or reactive.

Aza manao toy ny akoho, mahita vovonana.

Do not act like a chicken, seeing only the eggs.

Be aware of the consequences of your actions and the impact they have on others.

Aza manao toy ny akoho, tsy mba mahay manambaka.

Do not be like the chicken, who doesn't know how to climb.

Embrace growth and self-improvement, rather than remaining stagnant or limited.

Aza manao toy ny akoho, tsy mba mahay mitondra.

Do not be like the chicken, who doesn't know how to lead.

Be a strong and effective leader, rather than simply following others.

Aza manao toy ny akoho, tsy mba misy fahamarinana.

Do not be like the chicken, there is no truth

Be wise and thoughtful in your actions, rather than impulsive or reactive.

Aza manao toy ny akoho, tsy mba misy fanahy.

Do not be like the chicken, there is no spirit.

Be wise and thoughtful in your actions, rather than impulsive or reactive.

Aza manao toy ny anatra, tsy mba mahay manambara.

10

Do not be like the duck, who doesn't know how to proclaim.

Don't be like a duck that cannot express itself or communicate effectively.

Aza manao toy ny fitaratra, tsy mba misy loza.

Do not be like the dew, there is no harm.

Be adaptable and flexible, as this can lead to a smoother journey through life.

Aza manao toy ny fotsy manan-kavana.

Do not act like a white cloth with a stain.

Do not pretend to be perfect when you have flaws.

Aza manao toy ny fotsy, tsy mba mahay mananatra.

Do not be like the white, who doesn't know how to sew.

Embrace growth and self-improvement, rather than remaining stagnant or limited.

Aza manao toy ny hazo manan-karena, tsy mifanaraka.

Do not act like a rich tree, not getting along.

Do not let wealth or success cause division or conflict.

Aza manao toy ny hazo, tsy mba misy loza.

Do not be like the tree, there is no harm.

Be adaptable and flexible, as this can lead to a smoother journey through life.

Aza manao toy ny hazondamosina,

manjary akondro.

Do not act like a banana tree that becomes a sugar cane.

Do not pretend to be someone you are not.

Aza manao toy ny kanto, tsy mba misy loza.

Do not be like the corner, there is no harm.

Adapt to your surroundings and circumstances, rather than remaining rigid or stuck.

Aza manao toy ny kely, tsy mba mahay manambaka.

Do not be like the small, who doesn't know how to climb.

Embrace growth and self-improvement, rather than remaining stagnant or limited.

Aza manao toy ny kirihitra tsy mba mihavaka.

Do not be like the wall that never cracks.

Be open to change and willing to adapt to new situations.

Aza manao toy ny mpanao, tsy mba mahay mitady.

Do not be like the doer, who doesn't know how to search

Embrace growth and self-improvement, rather than remaining stagnant or limited.

Aza manao toy ny olona, tsy mba misy fahendrena.

Do not be like the people, there is no wisdom.

Be wise and thoughtful in your actions,

rather than blindly following others.

Aza manao toy ny ondry manan-karena, tsy mifanaraka.

Do not act like a rich sheep, not getting along.

Do not let wealth or success cause division or conflict.

Aza manao toy ny ondry tsy mba mahafinaritra.

Do not be like the sheep that never pleases.

Always strive to be helpful and pleasing to others.

Aza manao toy ny rano maty, tsy mba misy fahendrena.

Do not be like the dead water, there is no

wisdom.

Be wise and adaptable, as this can lead to a smoother journey through life.

Aza manao toy ny rano maty, tsy mba misy loza.

Do not be like the dead water, there is no harm.

Be adaptable and go with the flow, as this can

Aza manao toy ny rano mifoka, tsy mba misy loza.

Do not be like boiling water, there is no harm.

Remain calm and composed in difficult situations, as this can lead to better outcomes.

Aza manao toy ny rano, tsy mba misy fahamarinana.

Do not be like the water, there is no truth.

Be honest and genuine in your actions and intentions, rather than being deceptive or manipulative.

Aza manao toy ny rano, tsy mba misy loza.

Do not be like the water, there is no harm.

Be adaptable and go with the flow, as this can lead to a smoother journey

Aza manao toy ny rivotra, tsy mba mahalala ny mitsoka.

Do not be like the wind, which doesn't know where it's going

Be purposeful and deliberate in your actions, rather than being aimless or directionless.

Aza manao toy ny rivotra, tsy mba misy faritra.

Do not be like the wind, there is no boundary.

Be adaptable and flexible, as this can lead to success and growth in many areas of life.

Aza manao toy ny rivotra, tsy mba misy loza.

Do not be like the wind, there is no harm.

Be adaptable and flexible, as this can lead to a smoother journey through life.

Aza manao toy ny solom-bavàna, tsy mba misy fahamarinana.

Do not be like the empty words, there is no

truth.

Be honest and truthful in your words and actions, rather than deceptive or insincere.

Aza manao toy ny solon-tsodina, tsy mba misy fahendrena.

Do not be like the fallen branch, there is no wisdom.

Embrace growth and self-improvement, rather than remaining stagnant or limited.

Aza manao toy ny tandroka manan-karena, tsy mifanary.

Do not act like a rich basket, not sharing.

Be generous and share your wealth or knowledge with others.

Aza manao toy ny tandroka tsy mba mahafinaritra.

Do not be like the basket that never pleases.

Always strive to be helpful and pleasing to others.

Aza manao toy ny trondro, tsy mba misy loza.

Do not be like the fish, there is no harm

Be adaptable and go with the flow, as this can lead to a smoother journey through life.

Aza manao toy ny vahoaka, tsy mba misy fahendrena.

Do not be like the people, there is no wisdom.

Be wise and thoughtful in your actions, rather than blindly following others.

Aza manao toy ny vao, tsy mba misy fanahy.

Do not be like the new, there is no spirit.

Embrace the wisdom of the past and respect traditions and customs.

Aza manao toy ny vao, tsy mba misy hery.

Do not be like the new, there is no strength.

Embrace the wisdom of the past and respect traditions and customs.

Aza manao toy ny vato voatavo, tsy mifankahazo.

Do not be like the stone that cannot be split, not getting along.

Be flexible and willing to compromise for the sake of harmony.

Aza manao toy ny vato, tsy mba misy loza.

Do not be like the stone, there is no harm.

Be adaptable and flexible, as this can lead to a smoother journey through life.

Aza manao toy ny volamena manan-karena, tsy mifanaraka.

Do not act like rich gold, not getting along.

Do not let wealth or success cause division or conflict.

Aza manao toy ny volana, tsy mba misy loza.

Do not be like the moon, there is no harm.

Be adaptable and change with the times, as this can lead to a smoother journey through life.

Aza manao zavatra tsy ampy, fa ny tsy ampy no mahatsiravina.

Do not do things halfway, for it is the incomplete that is disgraceful.

Always strive to complete tasks to the best of your ability.

Aza miaina amin'ny fitiavana ka tsy mahita izay ho avy.

Don't be so in love that you can't tell when rain is coming.

Don't let love blind you to reality or potential problems.

Aza mitady vato hahazoan'ny rano, fa izay eny am-paosy no atolotra.

Do not look for stones to hold water, give what is within the fence.

Make the most of the resources and opportunities available to you.

Aza miteniteny manao, fa manao.

Do not talk about doing, but do.

Actions speak louder than words.

Aza mitsahatra mitady vato hahazoan'ny vadina, fa izay eny am-paosy no atolotra.

Do not keep searching for stones to please your spouse, give what is within the fence.

Focus on providing for your loved ones with what you have available.

Efa lavo ilay vorona, saingy tsy misy afo hahafahana manomboka azy.

You may well have caught a bird, but have

you a fire to roast it on?

It's important to have the resources or means to make the most of an opportunity.

Ento tanana ilay valiha, fa ento nofy ny feony.

You can catch a cricket in your hand but its song is all over the field.

Some things have a wider impact or influence beyond their immediate presence.

Eritrereto ny lavitra, tsy hitany ny orona.

Distracted by what is far away, he does not see his nose.

Focusing too much on distant goals or issues may cause one to neglect immediate concerns or problems.

Fady be dia lavitra, ny fady tsy

mahafinaritra.

A great taboo is far away, a small taboo is not pleasant.

Respect the customs and traditions of others, even if they seem strange or unfamiliar.

Fihavanana madio, tsy mba hisy ratsy.

With a strong sense of community, there is no room for evil

This proverb emphasizes the idea that a strong community based on mutual respect, support, and kindness can prevent the spread of negativity and harm.

Izy avy any amin'ny lafo be dia sakafo iray ihany.

From all the fish in the pot, you can only make one soup.

Different elements can come together for a single outcome.

Mampihinàna vorona mihitsy ny firenena.

Govern a country as you would roast a crocodile on a spit.

Rule with care and attention to detail.

Miarahaba tsy mandehandeha.

Welcoming is not going anywhere

This proverb suggests that once a relationship has been established, it should be maintained through continued kindness and generosity.

Misy ny tsiny, tsy misy ny tody; ka ny fihavanana no maha-izy antsika.

There may be differences, but there is no

enmity; that is the essence of our unity

This proverb emphasizes the idea that differences and disagreements may exist within a community, but it is through a spirit of solidarity and understanding that those differences can be resolved and overcome.

Na izay tanana no resy dia ny tena no marary.

Whichever hand is cut, the whole body feels the pain.

Problems affect the entire community or family.

Na kely aza ny sakafo, hifanampy isika na dia valala iray aza.

However little food we have, we'll share it even if it's only one locust.

No matter how little we have, we should be willing to share with others in need.

**Na ny maty aza tia tsy misy foana ny
toerana miasa amin'ny fianakaviana.**

*Even the dead in their family vaults enjoy
being in large company.*

People appreciate and cherish being a part
of a larger community, even after death.

Ny adala an-tanàna dia adala.

The fool in the city is still a fool.

A person's nature doesn't change just
because their surroundings change.

**Ny adala no ampiasaina, fa tsy ny ratsy
adala.**

The fool is used, not the malicious fool.

People may take advantage of the naive or
gullible, but not those who are intentionally

harmful.

Ny adala tsy maty am-pandriana, fa maty am-pandeha.

The fool doesn't die sitting down, but dies standing up.

Foolish actions and decisions can lead to disastrous outcomes.

Ny adala tsy mba mahay mitady.

The fool does not know how to search.

Foolish people often lack the initiative or persistence to seek opportunities or solutions.

Ny adala tsy mba mividy ny mpanao zavatra.

The fool does not buy the doer.

Foolish people do not appreciate the value of hard work and skilled individuals.

Ny adala tsy mba mividy ny soa.

The fool does not buy the good.

Foolish people often fail to recognize or invest in what is truly valuable.

Ny adala tsy mba mividy ny tany.

The fool does not buy the land.

Foolish people often make poor decisions and miss out on valuable opportunities.

Ny aina tsy misy ny, fa ny olona.

Life has no taste, but the people do.

People create their own experiences and perceptions, which can vary widely.

Ny akoho tsy mba mandeha, fa ny voalavo.

The chicken doesn't go, but the rat does.

Some people avoid responsibility while others take action and make things happen.

Ny ala atao hoe: ala.

The forest is said to be a forest.

Respect and preserve nature, as it provides for our needs.

Ny ala ato no tapaka, ny ala ato no hatakana.

The forest here is cut down, the forest here is held back.

The forest from where one cuts wood is also the forest that provides shade, emphasizing the importance of addressing issues and challenges as they occur in their current context and taking action to prevent them from escalating further.

Ny ala tsy mba mahavoky ny tanana.

The forest does not satisfy the hand.

Material possessions cannot always bring happiness or fulfillment.

Ny ala tsy mba mividy ny hazo.

The forest does not buy the trees.

The environment is a result of the individual components that make it up.

Ny ala tsy mba mividy ny tany.

The forest does not buy the land.

The natural world cannot provide for our

needs without our effort and care.

Ny ala tsy mba mividy ny vahoaka.

The forest does not buy the people.

Nature and its resources are not solely responsible for our well-being; human effort and cooperation are also necessary.

Ny alika mihodina tsy mitondra hery, fa mitondra tahotra.

The barking dog gives you no power — it gives you fear.

Aggressive or intimidating behavior may not bring strength or respect, but instead provoke fear and anxiety.

Ny alika tsy mainty no maty laza.

Only thin dogs become wild.

People who lack resources or support are more likely to act out or resort to desperate measures.

Ny aloka tsy misy toa, fa ny olona.

The light has no comparison, but the people do.

People have different talents and abilities that can be compared and appreciated.

Ny anana tsy misy tsinay, fa ny vokatra.

The pineapple has no leaves, but the fruit.

Focus on the results and outcomes rather than appearances.

Ny anatra tsy mba mahavoky ny vokatra.

The duck does not satisfy the fruit.

Results and accomplishments cannot be

achieved without effort and perseverance.

Ny anatra tsy mba mifindra, fa ny vokatra.

The duck does not change, but the fruit does.

Adaptability and growth come from the results of our actions and decisions.

Ny andriana tsy mba maina, fa ny vahoaka.

The nobles are never thirsty, but the people are.

Those in power often

Ny andro tsy mba mividy ny volana.

The day does not buy the month.

Short-term achievements or successes do

not guarantee long-term stability or
progress.

**Ny ankizy tsy mba mividy ny
ankohonana.**

The children do not buy the family.

Relationships and bonds are more
important than material possessions or
wealth.

Ny ankizy tsy mba mividy ny raharaha.

The children do not buy the affair.

Children should not be burdened with adult
responsibilities or concerns.

**Ny ankohonana tsy mba mividy ny
raharaha.**

The family does not buy the affair.

Family bonds and relationships are more important than material possessions or wealth.

Ny antsasaka tsy mahita valimbabena.

The grasshopper cannot see the locust.

People often cannot see their own faults or shortcomings.

Ny antso miala am-paosy tsy mahazo tsiron'ondry.

The call from outside the fence does not get the sheep's attention.

It is difficult to influence others from a distance or without direct involvement.

Ny atao raha tiana, tsy azo atakalo.

What is done out of love cannot be undone.

Love leads to actions that are difficult to change or take back.

Ny atao tsy misy fitarainana.

What is done has no complaints.

Accept the consequences of your actions without complaining.

Ny atody tsy miady amin'ny vato.

An egg does not fight a rock.

Avoid engaging in conflicts or competitions where you are at a significant disadvantage or where the outcome is clearly unfavorable.

Ny aty amin'ny lafiny tsy mba midika, fa ny any amin'ny andro.

What's in the shadow doesn't show, but what's in the light does.

Actions and intentions are revealed through time and experience.

Ny aty amin'ny lovana no mba mahatonga ny masoandro.

The sun is caused by the heart of the sky.

Everything in life is interconnected and has a cause.

Ny aty amin'ny lovana no mba mahatonga ny volana.

The moon is caused by the heart of the sky.

Everything in life is interconnected and has a cause.

Ny aty amin'ny tantely no misy ny tarehy.

The beauty is in the honeycomb.

True beauty and value are often found in unexpected places.

Ny biby tsy mahay hifanaraka, ny olona tsy mahay hifampaherezana.

The animals that can't get along, the people that can't coexist.

Peace and harmony come from mutual understanding and cooperation.

Ny boky tsy mba mangidy, fa ny tanana.

The book does not bite, but the hand does.

Knowledge and learning are essential, but they must be applied and acted upon to have an impact.

Ny boky tsy mba misy toto, fa ny amboara.

The book has no blood, but the pen does.

Words and knowledge have the power to create or destroy.

Ny dilo no mividy ny olona.

The water buys the people.

Relationships and connections are often built through shared experiences and hardships.

Ny doro mampiray, fa ny sabatra mampisaraka.

The door brings together, but the thorn separates.

Relationships are built through openness and communication, while conflict and misunderstandings can drive people apart.

Ny doro tsy mba mifidy ny havoana.

The door doesn't choose the weather.

Life is unpredictable, and we must be prepared to face challenges and adapt.

Ny fahadalana dia mitambatra, ka hitraka amin'ny fahoriana.

Idleness moves so slowly that it will be overtaken by misery.

Laziness or inactivity can lead to negative consequences.

Ny fahafatesana tsy mba mifidy ny olona.

Death doesn't choose people.

Death is inevitable and affects everyone, regardless of their status or background.

Ny fahagola tsy mba mahavoky ny

soavaly.

The galloping does not satisfy the horse.

Effort and persistence are necessary for success and accomplishment.

Ny fahamarinana tsy mba mividy ny hazo.

The truth does not buy the tree.

Truth and honesty cannot always solve every problem or secure every resource.

Ny fahamarinana tsy misy toa, fa ny olona.

The truth has no comparison, but the people do.

People's perceptions of the truth can vary, but the truth itself remains constant.

Ny faharetana tsy mba mahavoky ny fahoriana.

Perseverance does not satisfy the suffering.

Overcoming difficulties requires effort and resilience.

Ny fahasoavana tsy mba mahavoky ny olona.

The grace does not satisfy the people.

Spiritual and moral wealth cannot bring happiness to everyone.

Ny fahasoavana tsy mba mividy ny fahendrena.

The grace does not buy the wisdom

Spiritual wealth and moral virtues cannot be purchased or acquired through material means.

Ny fahasoavana tsy mba mividy ny vola.

The grace does not buy the money.

Spiritual and moral wealth cannot be purchased with material wealth.

Ny fahatsiarovana tsy misy tsihy, fa ny olona.

Memory has no laughter, but the people do.

People create their own memories and shared experiences.

Ny fanahy tsy mba mahavoky ny tany.

The spirit does not satisfy the land.

Spiritual and moral wealth cannot provide for our material needs.

Ny fanahy tsy mba mihidy vava, fa ny vavaka.

The spirit doesn't close the mouth, but the prayer does.

Spiritual growth and connection require action and effort, not just words.

Ny fanahy tsy mba mividy ny tanana.

The spirit does not buy the body.

Material possessions cannot bring true happiness or spiritual fulfillment.

Ny fanahy tsy mba mizaka, fa ny nofo.

The soul doesn't carry, but the body does.

The physical body bears the burdens and challenges of life.

Ny fanahy tsy misy hazon'omby.

The spirit has no cattle pen.

The human spirit cannot be confined or limited.

Ny fandroana tsy mba mivadika, fa ny fano.

The rice doesn't turn, but the water does.

Change and progress are brought about by external forces and circumstances.

Ny feon'ny alika tsy hery, fa tahotra.

The dog's bark is not might, but fright.

Aggressive or intimidating behavior may not bring strength or respect, but instead provoke fear and anxiety.

Ny fiainana toy ny hazo tsy mba mafy.

Life is like a tree, never firm.

Life is unpredictable and constantly changing.

Ny fiainana toy ny sira, misy miakatra, misy midina.

Life is like a rope, some go up, some go down.

Life is full of ups and downs, successes, and failures.

Ny fiainana toy ny tandroka tsy mba misy farany.

Life is like a basket with no end.

Life is a never-ending journey filled with new experiences and challenges.

Ny fiainana toy ny taviboary, misy miorina, misy miova.

Life is like a game of checkers, some rise, some change.

Life is full of changes, successes, and failures.

Ny fiarahamonina dia man reminds azy momba ny ray, ny fitiavana kosa momba ny reny.

Friendship reminds us of fathers, love of mothers.

Friendship offers guidance and protection like a father, while love offers care and nurturing like a mother.

Ny fihavanana no maha-izy antsika.

Our unity is what makes us strong

This proverb emphasizes the importance working together and supporting each other, so that the community can overcome challenges and achieve their goals.

Ny fihavanana tsy mba lany andro.

Friendship never runs out of days.

True friendship and bonds last a lifetime.

Ny fihaviana tsy mba mihidy vava, fa ny vavaka.

Kindness doesn't close the mouth, but the prayer does.

Actions speak louder than words; genuine kindness and compassion should be shown through deeds.

Ny fihaviana tsy mba misy faritra.

Kindness has no region.

Kindness should be extended to everyone, regardless of their background or location.

Ny fihaviana tsy misy fandihizana.

Kindness has no boundaries.

Goodness and kindness should be
extended to everyone, without exception.

Ny fihaviana tsy misy harona.

Kindness has no fence.

Kindness should be extended to everyone
without boundaries.

**Ny fitiavana toy ny fanahy, tsy mba
mahita.**

Love is like the spirit, it cannot be seen.

Love is an intangible and powerful force
that cannot be measured or quantified.

Ny fo tsy mandry, ny maso tsy mahalala.

The heart doesn't sleep, the eyes don't recognize.

Emotions and feelings can be hidden, and people may not always understand what's happening beneath the surface.

Ny fo tsy mba mividy ny vola.

The heart does not buy the money.

True love and affection cannot be purchased with wealth.

Ny fon'ny lalàna tsy mandry, fa mandry ny fon'ny fanahy.

The noise of the law does not sleep, but the noise of the conscience does.

This proverb emphasizes the importance of one's conscience over the law. It suggests that while laws may be enforced and constantly remind people of their obligations, it is ultimately the individual's conscience that determines whether they will act morally and ethically.

Ny fotsy tsy mba mividy ny maina.

The white does not buy the stain.

Appearances and superficial traits cannot always bring true happiness or success.

Ny fotsy tsy mba mividy ny vazana.

The white does not buy the good pot.

Appearances and superficial traits cannot bring true happiness or success.

Ny fotsy tsy mba mividy ny vola.

The white does not buy the money.

Appearances and superficial traits cannot

bring true wealth or success.

Ny hafanana tsy mba mifindra.

Warmth does not change.

Genuine kindness and affection are
constant and unwavering.

**Ny hafanana tsy mba mipetraka
am-pandriana.**

Warmth doesn't stay sitting down.

Comfort and ease are fleeting and must be
actively maintained.

Ny hafanana tsy mba mividy ny vazana.

Warmth does not buy the good pot.

Comfort and happiness cannot always be
bought with material possessions.

Ny harena tsy mba mividy ny soa.

Wealth does not buy goodness.

Money cannot buy virtues like kindness, loyalty, or happiness.

Ny harona tsy mba mahavoky ny trano.

The pillar does not satisfy the house.

One individual's efforts are not enough to ensure the success or stability of a larger group.

Ny havana tsy mba mianjera, fa ny vavaka.

Relatives do not gather, but the prayers do.

Strong family bonds are built through shared faith and values.

Ny hazo maty tsy mba mitsoka, fa ny rano.

The dead tree doesn't grow, but the water does.

Change and growth come from nurturing and support.

Ny hazo tsy mba mahavoky ny hazo.

The tree does not satisfy the tree.

Material possessions cannot always bring happiness or fulfillment.

Ny hazo tsy mba mahavoky ny rano.

The tree does not satisfy the water.

Material possessions cannot always bring happiness or fulfillment.

Ny hazo tsy mba mahavoky ny vato.

The tree does not satisfy the stone.

Material possessions cannot always bring happiness or fulfillment.

Ny hazo tsy mba mahay mifindra.

The tree does not know how to move.

Being adaptable and open to change is an important aspect of personal growth.

Ny hazo tsy mba misy trosa.

The tree does not have a branch.

Everything has limitations and boundaries.

Ny hazo tsy mba mitsoka, fa ny rano no mihazona.

The tree doesn't grow, but the water supports it.

Growth and success are dependent on nurturing and support.

Ny hazo tsy mba mividy ny saina.

The tree does not buy the mind.

Material possessions cannot replace knowledge and intelligence.

Ny hazo tsy mba mividy ny tany.

The tree does not buy the land.

Material possessions cannot always secure long-term stability or resources.

Ny jamba tsy mba miaraka amin'ny lamba.

The strong don't walk with the weak.

People tend to associate with those who

share their interests and values.

Ny kely tsy mba mahavoky ny be.

The small does not satisfy the large.

It takes a collective effort to meet the needs of a larger group.

Ny kintana tsy mahazo volon'omby.

The stars cannot catch the cow's hair.

Some things are out of reach, no matter how hard we try.

Ny kintana tsy mba mila vola, fa ny masoandro.

The stars don't need money, but the sun does.

Different situations call for different resources and approaches.

Ny kirihitatra tsy mba manaja ny olona.

The needle doesn't respect people.

Small things can cause great discomfort or pain.

Ny kirihitra tsy miandry ny vola.

The drum does not wait for money.

Time waits for no one, and opportunities may pass if not seized.

Ny lalana maharitra, ny soa tsy mba maharitra.

The path is long, but the good doesn't last.

Good fortune and happiness can be fleeting, so it's important to appreciate them while they last.

Ny lalana tsy mba misy fahotana.

The path does not have sins.

Mistakes and missteps are a natural part of the journey through life.

Ny lalàna tsy mba mividy ny olona.

The law doesn't buy the people.

Rules and regulations cannot force genuine loyalty or respect.

Ny lamba tsy misy tsitsina.

The cloth without knots.

A situation without complications or problems.

Ny lova tsy mba mihavolana, fa ny toetra.

The treasure doesn't turn around, but the character does.

A person's character is more important than their material possessions.

Ny lovia maty tsy azo alaina, fa ny lovia velona.

A dead crab cannot be taken, but a living crab can.

Focus on what can be done and achieved rather than dwelling on past failures.

Ny lovia tsy mba manan-koditra.

The water jar has no lid.

Secrets and hidden truths often come to light eventually.

Ny loza tsy mba mividy ny harena.

The misfortune does not buy the wealth.

Wealth cannot protect us from all challenges or difficulties.

Ny loza tsy mba mividy ny soa.

The harm does not buy the good.

Negative actions and choices cannot lead to positive outcomes.

Ny loza tsy mba mividy ny soavaly.

The misfortune does not buy the horse

Wealth cannot protect us from all challenges or difficulties.

Ny loza tsy mba mividy ny tombontsoa.

The harm does not buy the benefit.

Difficulties and challenges can lead to personal growth and positive outcomes.

Ny mafana tsy mba mividy ny vazana.

The hot does not buy the good pot.

Intense emotions or passions cannot always bring happiness or fulfillment.

Ny mahantra tsy mividy tany.

The poor do not buy land.

Poverty often limits opportunities for growth and success.

Ny mahay mihinàna no mihina.

Those who know how to swim are the ones who sink.

Overconfidence can lead to failure.

Ny mahazoana dia tsy mba tongotra voalavo.

Those who rush things too much, without reflection, can be surpassed by those who take their time.

Patience and thoughtfulness can lead to better outcomes than haste and impulsiveness.

Ny malemy ny vovoka no maty ny vorona.

It is the softness of the lime that is fatal to the bird.

Danger can lurk in seemingly harmless situations or things.

Ny maso no miandry, fa ny vavaka no manery.

The eyes wait, but the prayers encourage.

Patience and faith will often bring about the desired outcome.

Ny masoandro tsy mahita ny kintana.

The sun doesn't see the stars.

People often fail to see the beauty in others when they are focused on their own achievements.

Ny masoandro tsy mba mividy ny vola.

The sun does not buy the money

Material wealth cannot buy everything, especially intangible qualities like happiness or enlightenment.

Ny masoandro tsy mba mividy ny volana.

The sun does not buy the moon.

Some things in life are beyond our control and cannot be bought or influenced.

Ny mpanankarena tsy misy fahotana.

The rich have no sins.

Wealthy people often get away with things that others cannot.

Ny mpanao zavatra tsy ampy no mahatsiravina.

The one who does things incompletely brings disgrace upon themselves.

Always strive to complete tasks to the best of your ability to avoid failure or shame.

Ny mpanjaka mianjera dia noho ny olona; ny renirano manankavana dia noho ny vato.

When the king reigns it is thanks to the people; when a river sings it's thanks to the stones.

Leadership and success depend on the support of others.

Ny olona tsy mahay manaja tsy mahita tsara.

People who don't know how to respect don't see good.

Disrespectful people often miss out on valuable opportunities and relationships.

Ny olona tsy mba mividy ny harena.

The people do not buy the wealth

Wealth cannot buy everything, especially intangible qualities like loyalty or happiness.

Ny olona tsy mba mividy ny hazo.

The people do not buy the tree.

Community and cooperation are essential for a successful society.

Ny olona tsy mba mividy ny soa.

The people do not buy the good.

Goodness and virtue come from within, not from external forces.

Ny olona tsy mba mividy ny tany.

The people do not buy the land

Community

Ny omby dia hahazo, fa ny lainga dia hahavita.

The end of an ox is beef, and the end of a

lie is grief.

Lies lead to negative consequences.

Ny rano masina tsy atolotra an'Ala.

Holy water is not given to the forest.

Do not waste valuable resources on futile efforts.

Ny rano mavitrika tsy mba mahafinaritra.

Polluted water is not pleasing.

Corruption and dishonesty are undesirable and bring negative consequences.

Ny rano tsy mahery no manakana ny lalana.

It's not the strong water that blocks the path.

71

Obstacles can be overcome with determination and perseverance.

Ny rano tsy mba mahavoky ny rano.

The water does not satisfy the water.

Material possessions cannot always bring happiness or fulfillment.

Ny rano tsy mba mahavoky ny vato.

The water does not satisfy the stone.

Material possessions cannot always bring happiness or fulfillment.

Ny rano tsy mba miaina, fa ny olona no miaina.

The water doesn't live, but the people do.

People give life and meaning to the world around them.

Ny rano tsy mba mividy ny angovo.

Water does not buy the source.

Resources and opportunities cannot guarantee success without effort.

Ny rano tsy mba mividy ny hazo.

The water does not buy the tree

Our environment and circumstances cannot protect us from all challenges or difficulties.

Ny rano tsy mba mividy ny loza.

The water does not buy the harm.

Our environment and circumstances cannot protect us from all challenges or difficulties.

Ny rano tsy mba mividy ny rivotra.

The water does not buy the wind.

Some things in life cannot be controlled or purchased, no matter how much we might desire them.

Ny rano tsy mba mividy ny tany.

Water does not buy the land.

Resources and opportunities cannot guarantee success without effort and care.

Ny rano tsy mba mividy ny tody.

The water does not buy the nail.

Our environment and circumstances cannot protect us from all challenges or difficulties.

Ny rano tsy mba mividy ny vahoaka.

The water does not buy the people

Our environment cannot bring people together or create community without our effort and care.

Ny rano tsy misy rivotra, fa ny olona.

The water has no wind, but the people do.

People create their own movement and change in life.

Ny ranomasina tsy mba mahavoky ny samby.

The sea does not satisfy the shore.

There is a natural balance and harmony in life that must be maintained.

Ny ranomasina tsy mba misy solafaka.

The sea never runs out of fish.

Opportunities and resources are abundant if you know where to look.

Ny ratsy tsy mba miala, fa ny soa.

The bad doesn't leave, but the good does.

It's easier to focus on the negative aspects of life rather than the positive.

Ny saha atao valimpitaka.

The field is turned into a notebook.

Make use of the resources you have to achieve your goals.

Ny saina tsy mba mividy ny hazo.

The mind does not buy the wood.

Knowledge and intelligence cannot replace practical skills and experience.

Ny saina tsy mba mividy ny maina.

The mind does not buy the stain.

Wisdom and intelligence cannot erase past mistakes or wrongdoings.

Ny saina tsy mba mividy ny vavàna.

The mind does not buy the mouth.

Words alone cannot capture the depth and complexity of our thoughts and emotions.

Ny sakafo mihinana tsy misy tory, fa ny olona no matory.

The food eaten has no bed, but the people sleep.

People need rest and recovery, even after satisfying their basic needs.

Ny sakafo tsy mba misy ny, fa ny olona.

The food doesn't have a taste, but the people do.

People create their own experiences and perceptions, which can vary widely.

Ny sakafo tsy mba misy voafaritra.

The meal has no boundaries.

Generosity and sharing should extend to everyone, without discrimination.

Ny sakafo tsy mba mividy ny toaka.

The food does not buy the alcohol.

It is important to prioritize and balance our needs and desires.

Ny sakafo tsy mba mividy ny vokatra.

The food does not buy the fruit.

Results and accomplishments come from hard work and perseverance, not just from being well-fed or comfortable.

Ny sasak'alina tsy mba mahavoky ny masoandro.

The darkness of night does not satisfy the daylight.

Difficult times are a part of life and will eventually give way to brighter moments.

Ny sira tsy mba mahavoky ny tanana.

The rope does not satisfy the hand.

Material possessions cannot always bring happiness or fulfillment.

Ny sira tsy mba mifindra, fa ny vokatra.

The rope does not change, but the fruit does.

Adaptability and growth come from the results of our actions and decisions.

Ny soa atao, ny ratsy avokoa.

Good actions bring good results, and bad actions bring bad results.

You reap what you sow.

Ny soa tsy mba mividy ny ratsy.

The good does not buy the bad.

Good deeds and intentions cannot erase or counteract negative actions or consequences.

Ny tana tsy mba mivandravandra, fa ny olona.

The land doesn't move, but the people do.

Change comes from people, not from the environment.

Ny tanana tsy mba mahavoky ny lovia.

The hand does not satisfy the stomach.

Material possessions alone cannot bring happiness or fulfillment.

Ny tanana tsy mba mahavoky ny maso.

The hand does not satisfy the eye

Material possessions cannot always bring happiness or fulfillment.

Ny tanàna tsy mba mahavoky ny olona.

The town does not satisfy the people.

A successful community requires the effort

and cooperation of all its members

Ny tanàna tsy mba misy tombo, fa ny angovo.

The city has no holes, but the palm wine does.

There is always something to discover or learn, even in familiar places.

Ny tandroka tsy mba mividy ny velona.

The basket does not buy the living.

Material possessions cannot bring true happiness or fulfillment.

Ny tanora tsy mba mividy ny fahendrena.

Youth does not buy wisdom.

Wisdom comes from experience and age,

not from youthfulness.

**Ny tany dia manambady Andriamanitra -
mameno ny velona ary mamonjy ny
maty.**

*The earth is God's bride — she feeds the
living and cherishes the dead.*

The earth provides for all living things and
is a final resting place for the deceased.

**Ny tany no saribakoly, ny olona no
akoho.**

*The earth is a giant cooking pot and men
are the meat therein.*

The world is full of challenges and people
must navigate through them, often facing
difficulties.

Ny tany tsy mba mahantra, fa ny olona.

The land is never poor, but the people are.

Poverty is often a result of mismanagement or lack of knowledge.

Ny tany tsy mba mahavoky ny andriana.

The land does not satisfy the noble.

Social status and wealth do not guarantee happiness or fulfillment.

Ny tany tsy mba mahavoky ny harena.

The land does not satisfy the wealth.

Wealth cannot buy everything, especially intangible qualities like loyalty or happiness.

Ny tany tsy mba mahavoky ny olona.

The land does not satisfy the people.

Community and cooperation are essential
for a successful society.

Ny tany tsy mba mahay manomboka.

The land does not know how to start.

Initiative and progress come from the
people, not from the environment.

Ny tany tsy mba mahay mitsoka.

*The land does not know how to be
annoyed.*

Patience and resilience come from the
people, not from the environment.

Ny tany tsy mba mampiray ny lovia.

*The land doesn't bring the water jars
together.*

Certain things in life cannot be forced or

controlled.

Ny tany tsy mba manan-kavia.

The land has no master.

Nature is a force that cannot be controlled or tamed.

Ny tany tsy mba mangidy, fa ny olona.

The land doesn't bite, but the people do.

People are often the cause of problems, not the environment or circumstances.

Ny tany tsy mba mifangaro, fa ny olona no mifangaro.

The land does not mix, but the people mix

People are diverse and interact with one another, while the environment remains constant.

Ny tany tsy mba mifindra, fa ny olona.

The land does not change, but the people do.

People are responsible for the changes and developments that occur in the world around them.

Ny tany tsy mba mifindra, fa ny rano.

The land does not change, but the water does.

Our environment remains constant, while circumstances and situations change.

Ny tany tsy mba mila olona, fa ny olona no mila ny tany.

The land doesn't need people, but people need the land.

People rely on the environment for their survival and well-being.

Ny tany tsy mba mitsoka, fa ny rano.

The land does not grow, but the water does.

Growth and prosperity come from nurturing and support.

Ny tany tsy mba mividy ny ankizy.

The land does not buy the children.

The environment cannot provide for the needs of future generations without our care and stewardship.

Ny tany tsy mba mividy ny harena.

The land does not buy the wealth.

The environment cannot provide for our

needs without our effort and care.

Ny tany tsy mba mividy ny sakafo.

The land does not buy the food.

The environment cannot provide for our needs without our effort and care.

Ny tany tsy mba mividy ny soa.

The land does not buy the good.

The environment cannot provide for our needs without our effort and care.

Ny tany tsy mba mividy ny vola.

The land does not buy the money.

Wealth cannot purchase everything, especially intangible qualities like loyalty or happiness.

Ny tany tsy misy fasana, dia hita ao amin'ny tany mampihinam-bavy.

When you are looking for a country with no tombstones, you will find yourself in the land of cannibals.

Avoiding one problem can lead you to another, potentially worse, situation.

Ny tia ny lalàna dia vola very.

To love the law is to lose money.

Strict adherence to rules can be costly.

Ny tody tsy misy fatratra.

The spear without a sharp point.

A person without skills or talent is not effective.

Ny tody tsy misy lafatra.

The spear has no handle.

Some problems have no easy solution.

Ny tody tsy misy tsy misy velona.

There is no spear without life.

Every tool or resource has its purpose and value.

Ny toetr'andro tsy misy takon'omby.

The weather has no master.

This proverb highlights the unpredictability and uncontrollability of the weather, as a reminder that there are some things in life that are simply beyond human control, and we must accept and adapt to these natural occurrences.

Ny torohevitra dia vahiny; raha tiana dia mitoetra, raha tsy tiana dia mandositra.

Advice is a stranger; if he's welcome he stays for the night; if not, he leaves the same day.

The value of advice depends on whether it's accepted or rejected.

Ny tovovavy tsy mba mividy ny ranomasina.

The girl doesn't buy the sea.

Some things are beyond our control or influence.

Ny trosa no manao ny mpangalatra.

Debts make the thief.

Financial problems can lead to dishonesty.

Ny tsihy tsy mba mianjera, fa ny olona.

The laughter doesn't gather, but the people do.

People come together through shared experiences and joy.

Ny tsy ampy tsy mba mahavoky ny be.

Insufficiency does not satisfy the many.

It takes a collective effort to meet the needs of a larger group.

Ny tsy azo am-pandriana, azo am-pandeha.

What can't be done sitting down can be done standing up.

There is always a way to overcome obstacles and achieve your goals.

Ny tsy fantatra tsy mba mihantona.

The unknown doesn't stop.

Curiosity and the desire for knowledge are natural human instincts.

Ny vahoaka tsy mba mahavoky ny olona.

The people do not satisfy the individual.

It takes a collective effort to meet the needs and desires of every person.

Ny vahoaka tsy mba mahavoky ny tany.

The people do not satisfy the land

Community and cooperation are essential for a successful society.

Ny vahoaka tsy mba mividy ny fanjakana.

The people do not buy the government.

The support and loyalty of citizens cannot be bought; it must be earned through good governance.

Ny vahoaka tsy mba mividy ny tany, fa ny tany no mividy ny vahoaka.

The people don't buy the land, but the land buys the people.

Land and resources have the power to shape societies and people's lives.

Ny vahoaka tsy mba mividy ny tany.

The people do not buy the land.

Community and cooperation are essential for a successful society.

Ny varavara tsy mba miakatra.

The smoke doesn't rise.

Unproductive actions and decisions do not lead to progress or success.

Ny vavaka tsy mba mihidy vava.

Prayer doesn't close the mouth.

Prayer alone is not enough; action and effort are also required.

Ny vavàna tsy mba mahavoky ny loha.

The mouth does not satisfy the head.

Words alone cannot fulfill our intellectual needs; action and experience are also necessary.

Ny vavàna tsy mba mahavoky ny saina.

The mouth does not satisfy the mind.

Words alone cannot bring happiness or fulfillment; actions are necessary.

Ny vavàna tsy mba mividy ny saina.

The mouth does not buy the mind

Words alone cannot influence or change someone's thoughts or opinions; actions are necessary.

Ny vavàna tsy mba mividy ny vola.

The mouth does not buy the money.

Words alone cannot secure wealth or success; actions are necessary.

Ny vaventy tsy mba mividy ny rano.

The jar does not buy the water.

Some things in life are given freely and

cannot be bought or controlled.

Ny vazaha ny ankohonana.

The foreigner is the family.

Treat strangers with kindness and hospitality as if they were part of the family.

Ny vazana tsy mba mahavoky ny tanana.

The good pot does not satisfy the hand.

Material possessions cannot always bring happiness or fulfillment.

Ny vazana tsy mba mividy ny hafanana.

The good pot does not buy the warmth.

Material possessions cannot always bring happiness or comfort.

Ny vazana tsy mba mividy ny tany.

The good pot does not buy the land.

Material possessions cannot always bring happiness or fulfillment.

Ny velona tsy vokatra, ny maty tsy heloka.

Living is not a reward and dying is no crime.

Life and death are natural parts of existence and not matters of reward or punishment.

Ny vitsy tsy mahavoky ny maro.

The few do not satisfy the many.

A small effort is not enough to meet the needs of a larger group.

Ny vitsy tsy mahavoky ny tsirairay.

The few do not satisfy the individual.

It takes a collective effort to satisfy individual needs and desires.

Ny vitsy tsy mba mahafoy, fa ny maro.

A few do not satisfy, but many do.

Quantity matters in achieving satisfaction or success.

Ny vitsy tsy mba mahavoky ny be.

The few do not satisfy the many.

It takes a collective effort to meet the needs of a larger group.

Ny voa tsy mahandro, fa ny tandroka.

The fruit doesn't lie, but the basket does.

100

People may deceive you, but their actions will eventually reveal the truth.

Ny vokatra tsy mba mipetraka am-pandriana.

The fruit doesn't stay sitting down.

Progress and success require effort and action.

Ny vokatra tsy mba misy fototra, fa ny hazo.

The fruit has no base, but the tree does.

Results and outcomes depend on the foundations and support systems in place.

Ny vokatra tsy mba mividy ny angovo.

The fruit does not buy the tree.

Results and accomplishments cannot always secure long-term stability or resources.

Ny vokatra tsy mba mividy ny tany.

The fruit does not buy the land.

Results and accomplishments cannot always secure long-term stability or resources.

Ny vola no mividy ny lalàna.

Money buys the law.

Wealth and power can sometimes be used to manipulate or control the law.

Ny vola tsy mba mahavoky ny fahasahiranana.

Money does not satisfy the difficulty

Money cannot solve all problems or bring true happiness.

Ny vola tsy mba mipetraka an-tanety, fa ny vola no mipetraka an-tanety.

Money doesn't stay on the ground, but money stays on the ground.

Money is fleeting and can be lost or spent quickly.

Ny vola tsy mba mividy ny fahendrena.

Money does not buy wisdom.

Wealth cannot purchase true wisdom or knowledge, which must be gained through experience and learning.

Ny vola tsy mba mividy ny tany.

Money does not buy the land.

Wealth cannot buy everything, especially intangible qualities like loyalty or happiness.

Ny vola tsy mba mividy ny tody.

Money does not buy the spear.

Wealth cannot buy everything, especially intangible qualities like courage or determination.

Ny vola tsy mividy fitiavana.

Money can't buy love.

Genuine love and affection cannot be purchased with wealth.

Ny vola tsy mividy saina.

Money can't buy intelligence.

Wealth cannot purchase wisdom or

intelligence.

Ny volana tsy mba mitsabo.

The moon doesn't cure.

Some problems or issues cannot be
resolved with time alone.

Ny volana tsy mba mividy ny andro.

The month does not buy the day.

Long-term achievements or successes do
not guarantee short-term stability or
progress.

**Ny volana tsy mba mividy ny
masoandro.**

The moon does not buy the sun.

Some things in life are complementary and
cannot be replaced by one another.

Ny vorona mainty dia mainty amin'ny tany rehetra.

Crows are black everywhere.

Certain truths or characteristics remain constant, regardless of location or situation.

Ny zanaka no mampiray, fa ny vola no mampisaraka.

Children bring people together, but money separates them.

Relationships and bonds are often stronger through shared experiences, while wealth can create division.

Ny zanaka tsy mahay hihinana akondro dia izay amin'ny jamba no mihinana.

The child who doesn't know how to eat a banana eats with the peel.

Ignorance can lead to awkward or uncomfortable situations.

Ny zanaka tsy mba mifindra, fa ny vola.

The child does not change, but the money does.

Material wealth can be fleeting, while relationships and bonds are more constant.

Ny zava-mahery tsy mba mifanila.

Strong things do not resemble each other.

Strength and resilience come in many different forms.

Ny zavatra tsy mba mitsoka, fa ny olona.

Things do not grow, but people do.

Personal growth and development come

from within, not from external forces.

Ny zavatra tsy mba mividy ny olona.

Things do not buy people.

Material possessions cannot replace genuine relationships and connections.

Ny zaza kely tsy mahay mihinana, ny akoho tsy mahay mihinana koa.

The child who doesn't know how to eat is like a chicken that doesn't know how to eat.

Everyone must learn and grow at their own pace.

Ny zaza tsy mahay manam-paty dia ny amboara no mihinana.

The child who doesn't know how to eat yams eats the skin.

Lack of knowledge or experience can lead to making mistakes or poor decisions.

Ny zaza tsy mahay mandihy dia mihinana zaza.

The child who cannot dance says the other children are eating him.

People often blame others for their own shortcomings.

Ny zaza tsy mahay mandro, mihinana ny ondry.

The child who cannot herd sheep, eats them.

Those who lack skills may cause harm or waste valuable resources.

Ny zaza tsy mba mampiditra, fa ny fahasoavana.

The child doesn't enter, but the blessing does.

Children bring blessings and joy into people's lives.

Ny zaza tsy mba mifindra, fa ny fahasoavana.

The child does not change, but the grace of God does.

Goodness and virtue come from within and are influenced by divine grace, not external forces.

Ny zaza tsy mba mividy ny fahasoavana.

The child does not buy the grace.

Goodness and virtue are innate and cannot be purchased.

Ny zaza tsy mba mividy ny soa.

The child does not buy the good.

Children should not be burdened with adult responsibilities or concerns.

Ny zaza tsy mba mividy ny tany.

The child does not buy the land

Children should not be burdened with adult responsibilities or concerns.

Ny zaza tsy misy tahiry tsy mahay mamory.

The child without a plan doesn't know how to sweep.

Without a clear goal or plan, one cannot achieve success.

Ny zazalahy dia zazalahy ihany.

The child of a rat is a rat.

Children often resemble their parents.

Ohatra mihitsy ny lehilahy mitarika olona.

A man who lets his problems get the better of him is like the man who divorces his wife the first time she makes him angry.

Don't make hasty decisions based on emotions.

Raha mandeha ny voay, avy eo ny fosa.

When the crocodiles leave, the Caymans come.

Problems or difficulties can be replaced by other issues if not addressed properly.

Raha mandry ny rano, ny hazo tsy misy hafanana.

If the water dries up, the wood has no warmth.

Everything in life is interconnected and interdependent.

Raha matory ny tendrombohitra, dia voalavo ny valala.

If the hill is on fire the grasshoppers are roasted.

In difficult situations, even the seemingly insignificant may be affected.

Raha mitovy ny vokatra, tsy mahasoa ny hivarotra.

If the products are the same, there's no point in selling.

There is no need to compete when everyone offers the same thing.

Raha tsy hita maso, tsy mba mety atao.

If it's not seen, it's not done.

Actions and results are more important than words or intentions.

Raha tsy hita ny doro, dia tsy hita ny vovonana.

If you don't see the nest, you don't see the eggs.

To solve a problem, you must first understand its source.

Raha tsy misy ronono ny vato, tsy mahazo vidiny tsara ny tompony.

If the stone is not milky, its owner will generally not obtain the best price from it.

Quality and appearance matter when it comes to value.

Raha vaky vaky ny biby, ny sahalahy mihitsy no mihaino.

When the ducks are quacking, the frogs take it as a warning.

People should pay attention to signs or warnings from others.

Raha vao misy jirika, misy ny tsiron'akoho.

When there are drumbeats, there are chicken tails.

Excitement or activity often attracts attention and interest.

Raha vao misy ny manan-karena, misy ny mahantra.

Where there is wealth, there is poverty.

Wealth and poverty often coexist.

Rehefa tratrareo fakàna, dia izay no jerenao.

When you treat someone like a wild cat, he will steal your chickens.

Treat people poorly, and they may act poorly in return.

Rehefa tsy fantatra ny olona, dia inona no hampiasa.

Greet everyone cordially when you don't know who your in-laws are going to be.

Treat everyone with respect because you never know who you will be connected to in the future.

Tsara noho ny heloky ny olona noho ny heloky Andriamanitra.

Better to be guilty in the eyes of men than in the eyes of God.

It's better to face human judgment than to violate spiritual or moral principles.

Tsara ny vazana ny an-dranomasina.

The good pot is at the bottom of the sea.

The best things in life are often hidden or hard to find.

Tsara ny very vola fa tsy ny very namana.

Better to lose a little money than a little friendship.

Friendships are more important than material wealth.

Tsy azo omena kely valala raha tsy voalaka.

One can't give a grasshopper to a child if one has not caught it yet.

You cannot offer or promise something that you do not have or have not achieved.

Tsy handry ny menarana ny olona maty.

The dying person cannot wait for the shroud to be woven.

Urgent matters cannot be postponed.

Tsy mahita ny tany, fa ny varika.

Not seeing the land, but the frog.

Focus on the bigger picture rather than getting caught up in small details or distractions.

Tsy mahita ny vola, fa ny vohitra.

Not seeing the money, but the village.

Focus on the relationships and community rather than material wealth.

Tsy mahita tsiron'ondry ny an-tokan-tany.

The one inside the fence does not see the sheep's tail.

Sometimes we are too close to a situation to see it clearly.

Tsy mba maty ny manina.

The one who bends doesn't die.

Being flexible and adaptable can help you survive difficult situations.

Tsy mba miala an-tokan-tany ny onja.

The crab never leaves its hole.

People often stick to what they know and are comfortable with.

Tsy mba miandry vola, fa miandry tsiky.

Not waiting for money, but waiting for a smile.

Happiness and fulfillment often come from simple, intangible things rather than material wealth.

Tsy mihantsy irery ny vy.

Iron does not clang by itself.

People need others to make an impact or create meaningful change.

Tsy misy akoho tsy misy atody.

There is no chicken without an egg.

Everything has an origin or a cause.

Tsy misy aloka tsy misy fandriana.

There is no light without darkness.

Good times and bad times are part of life's natural cycle.

Tsy misy angatra tsy misy tody.

There is no claw without a nail.

Every action has a consequence, and every situation has its causes.

Tsy misy biby tsy mba misy hasina.

There is no animal without its usefulness.

Everyone and everything has a purpose and value.

Tsy misy fahafatesana tsy misy famonjena.

There is no death without salvation.

In every tragedy or loss, there is the potential for personal growth and renewal.

Tsy misy fahagola tsy misy sakay.

There is no galloping without a saddle.

You cannot achieve success without the necessary resources or tools.

Tsy misy fahagola tsy misy soavaly.

There is no galloping without a horse.

You cannot achieve success without the necessary resources or tools.

Tsy misy fahasoavana tsy misy fitsarana.

There is no grace without judgment.

Every action has consequences, and we must face them to learn and grow.

Tsy misy fahatsarana tsy misy fanantenana.

There is no improvement without hope.

Positive change requires belief in a better future.

Tsy misy fahavalo tsy misy fahazazana.

There is no enemy without a victory.

Every challenge or conflict offers the opportunity for growth and learning.

Tsy misy fahendrena tsy misy loza.

There is no wisdom without harm.

Wisdom and knowledge often come from overcoming challenges and difficulties.

Tsy misy fahoriana tsy misy valisoa.

There is no suffering without blessing.

Difficulties and challenges often bring valuable lessons and growth.

Tsy misy fahoriana tsy misy vokatra.

There is no suffering without fruit.

Hardship and struggle often lead to growth and positive outcomes.

Tsy misy fanahy tsy misy fo.

There is no spirit without heart.

Inner qualities such as love, compassion, and wisdom are essential for a fulfilling life.

**Tsy misy fandrosoana tsy misy
fanasana.**

*There is no progress without
encouragement.*

Support and encouragement are essential
for growth and development.

Tsy misy fararano ny manana.

There's no pond for the one who has.

Wealth and abundance often come to those
who already have plenty.

Tsy misy fihavanana tsy misy fitiavana.

There is no harmony without love.

Love and compassion are the foundations
of a peaceful and harmonious society.

Tsy misy fotsy izay tsy maitso.

There is no white without green.

There is good and bad in everything.

Tsy misy fotsy tsy misy maina.

There is no white without a stain.

No one is perfect; everyone has their flaws or weaknesses.

Tsy misy harena tsy misy akoholahy.

There is no wealth without a companion.

Success and abundance are best enjoyed when shared with others.

Tsy misy harena tsy misy faharetana.

There is no wealth without perseverance.

Success often requires determination and hard work.

Tsy misy harena tsy misy fahoriana.

There is no wealth without suffering.

Success often comes with its own set of challenges and hardships.

Tsy misy harena tsy misy fanahy.

There is no wealth without spirit.

True wealth comes from inner qualities such as integrity, kindness, and wisdom.

Tsy misy harena tsy misy vola.

There is no wealth without money.

Wealth and resources are often necessary for success and accomplishment.

Tsy misy havia tsy misy hiditra.

There is no fence without an entrance.

Every barrier or obstacle has a way to overcome it or navigate around it.

Tsy misy hazo feno, fa ny rivotra.

There is no full tree, only the wind.

No one is perfect; everyone has their flaws or weaknesses.

Tsy misy hazo mahatsara ny ankizy, fa ny fahasoavana.

No tree can make a child good, but the grace of God.

Goodness and virtue come from within, not from external forces.

Tsy misy hazo tsy misy tongotra.

There is no tree without roots.

Everything has a foundation or origin that supports its growth.

Tsy misy hazo tsy misy valimpitia.

There is no tree without shade.

Everything has its own set of benefits and drawbacks.

Tsy misy heloka izay tsy misy tambazotra.

There is no crime without a network.

Wrongdoing often involves a web of connections and relationships.

Tsy misy heloka tsy misy hadisoana.

There is no crime without a mistake.

Wrongdoing often arises from errors or poor judgment.

Tsy misy hery tsy misy fahoriana.

There is no strength without suffering

Strength and resilience often come from overcoming challenges and hardships.

Tsy misy hery tsy misy harena.

There is no strength without wealth.

Wealth and resources are often necessary for success and accomplishment.

Tsy misy hery tsy misy ratsy.

There is no strength without bad

Strength and resilience often come from overcoming challenges and difficulties.

Tsy misy hery tsy misy tady.

There is no strength without searching

Effort and persistence are necessary for success and accomplishment.

Tsy misy hery tsy misy vola.

There is no strength without money.

Wealth and resources are often necessary for success and accomplishment.

Tsy misy hifampitokisana izay tsy misy hifampiantranoana.

There is no trust without sharing a roof.

Trust is built through shared experiences and close relationships.

Tsy misy kanto tsy misy hazavana.

There is no corner without light.

There is always a solution or a way out of difficult situations.

Tsy misy kiraro tsy misy kely.

There is no big without a small.

Everything starts small before it grows.

Tsy misy lova tsy misy faty.

There is no treasure without death.

Great rewards often come with great risks or sacrifices.

Tsy misy loza izay tsy misy tombontsoa.

There is no harm without a benefit.

Every challenge or difficulty can teach us valuable lessons and lead to growth.

Tsy misy loza tsy misy tombontsoa.

There is no misfortune without a benefit.

Every challenge or difficulty can teach us valuable lessons and lead to growth.

Tsy misy maina tsy misy fotsy.

There is no stain without white.

No one is perfect; everyone has their flaws or weaknesses.

Tsy misy mangidy an'ny tany, fa ny tanana.

The land doesn't bite, but the hand does.

Our actions and choices have consequences, not the circumstances we are in.

Tsy misy mpiasa tsy misy farany.

There is no worker without an end.

Every task has an endpoint or goal to be achieved.

Tsy misy ny tsy misy ambin'ny angovo.

There is no fruit without the shelter of the tree.

Success and accomplishments come from a supportive environment and nurturing.

Tsy misy ny tsy misy angovo.

There is no fruit without a tree.

You cannot expect results without putting in

the effort.

Tsy misy ny tsy misy fahasoavana.

There is no life without grace.

Every life has its blessings and moments of happiness.

Tsy misy ny tsy misy fahotana.

There is no one without a sin

No one is perfect, and everyone makes mistakes or commits wrongdoings.

Tsy misy ny tsy misy soa.

There is no fruit without goodness

Goodness and virtue come from within, not from external forces.

Tsy misy ny tsy misy vokatra.

There is no tree without fruit

You cannot expect results without putting in the effort.

Tsy misy ny tsy misy, ny tsy misy tsy misy.

There is nothing that does not exist, what does not exist does not exist.

Everything has a purpose, and every situation or event has its place in the grand scheme of things.

Tsy misy ny tsy tonga saina.

There is nothing that doesn't come to mind.

Everything has a purpose or reason, even if it is not immediately apparent.

Tsy misy ny vao be, misy ny vao maro.

There is no big bamboo shoot without many bamboo shoots.

Success often comes from the collective efforts of many.

Tsy misy rà tsy misy vola.

There is no honey without money.

Success and achievement often require resources and investment.

Tsy misy rano tsy misy angovo.

There is no water without a source.

Everything has an origin or a cause.

Tsy misy rano tsy misy loza.

There is no water without harm.

Every resource or opportunity comes with its own set of challenges or risks.

Tsy misy rano tsy misy mihina.

There is no water without shallowness.

Every situation or resource has its limitations and weaknesses.

Tsy misy rano tsy misy rivotra.

There is no water without wind.

Everything in life is interconnected and influenced by other factors.

Tsy misy rano tsy misy samy.

There is no water without a source.

Everything has an origin or a cause.

138

Tsy misy rano tsy misy sira.

There is no water without a rope.

Every resource or opportunity comes with its own set of challenges or risks.

Tsy misy rano tsy misy vato.

There is no water without stones.

Obstacles and challenges are a natural part of life's journey.

Tsy misy ratsy tsy misy tsara, fihavanana ihany no mitondra.

There is no absolute good or absolute evil, it is only through solidarity that we can move forward

This proverb emphasizes the idea that there is no such thing as absolute good or evil, and that everything is relative. Only through the spirit of solidarity can we make progress and move forward.

Tsy misy ratsy tsy misy tsara.

There is no bad without good.

Every situation, no matter how difficult, has something positive to be found.

Tsy misy ravin-kazo tsy misy ravin-dratsy.

There is no forest without a bad path.

Life is filled with challenges and difficulties.

Tsy misy ravo tsy misy tandroka.

There is no honey without a basket.

Good things often require effort and patience to achieve.

Tsy misy rivotra tsy misy rahona.

There is no wind without dust.

With change and action come
consequences and repercussions.

Tsy misy roa tsy mifanakaiky.

*There are no two things that are not
related.*

Everything in life is interconnected.

Tsy misy saina tsy misy masoandro.

There is no mind without sunlight

Clarity and understanding come from
openness and enlightenment.

Tsy misy soa tsy misy ratsy.

There is no good without bad.

Good times and bad times are part of life's natural cycle.

Tsy misy tandroka tsy misy tsinay.

There is no basket without leaves.

Everything has a purpose or a use.

Tsy misy tany tsy misy fahoriana.

There is no land without suffering.

Life is full of challenges and difficulties, no matter where you are.

Tsy misy tany tsy misy lalàna.

There is no land without rules.

Rules and regulations are necessary for maintaining order and harmony.

Tsy misy tazomanga tsy misy solika.

There is no pot without a lid.

Every situation has a solution or a fitting response.

Tsy misy tendrombohitra tsy misy rano.

There is no mountain without water.

Challenges and difficulties often bring opportunities for growth and development.

Tsy misy tody tsy misy vazana.

There is no spear without a good pot.

Success requires the right tools and resources.

Tsy misy tokatranon'omby tsy misy

fototra.

There is no cow's tail without a base.

Everything has a foundation or origin

Tsy misy tokotaniny tsy misy oniny.

There is no fence without a post.

Every structure or system requires support and a foundation.

Tsy misy trano tsy misy aloka.

There is no house without light.

Every situation has a positive aspect or a silver lining.

Tsy misy trano tsy misy tandroka.

There is no house without a basket.

Every home requires basic necessities and resources.

Tsy misy tsinay izay tsy misy fototra.

There is no leaf without a base.

Everything has a foundation or starting point.

Tsy misy tsy akory tsy misy kintana.

There is no night without stars

Even in difficult times, there is always some light and hope.

Tsy misy tsy misy rano.

There is no fruit without water.

You cannot expect results without putting in the effort.

Tsy misy tsy misy zaza.

There is no fruit without a child.

The future is shaped by the actions and decisions of the younger generation.

Tsy misy vahoaka tsy misy fahendrena.

There is no people without wisdom.

Wisdom and knowledge are inherent in every community and culture.

Tsy misy varavarankely raha tsy misy rano.

There is no small puddle without water.

Small effects often have significant causes.

Tsy misy varavarankely tsy misy fahafatesana.

There is no small thorn without a death.

Even the smallest problems can have severe consequences if not addressed.

Tsy misy vitsy tsy misy be.

There is no small without a large.

Everything starts small before it grows.

Tsy misy vokatra tsy misy angatra.

There is no fruit without a branch.

You cannot expect results without putting in the effort and nurturing the process.

Tsy misy vokatra tsy misy angovo.

There is no fruit without a tree.

You cannot expect results without putting in

the effort.

Tsy misy vokatra tsy misy fahoriana.

There is no fruit without suffering.

Success often comes with its own set of challenges and hardships.

Tsy misy vokatra tsy misy harona.

There is no fruit without a fence.

Success and achievement require hard work and perseverance.

Tsy misy vola tsy misy hadisoana.

There is no money without a mistake.

Wealth often comes with its own set of challenges and negative consequences.

Tsy misy vola tsy misy ratsy.

There is no money without evil.

Money often comes with its own set of
challenges and negative consequences.

Tsy misy vola tsy misy tany.

There is no money without land

Wealth often comes from the resources and
opportunities provided by the environment.

Tsy misy volana tsy misy loza.

There is no month without harm.

Challenges and difficulties are a part of life
and can occur at any time.

Tsy misy volobe izay tsy mihena.

There is no big rat that doesn't get caught.

Even the most cunning or powerful may eventually face consequences for their actions.

Tsy misy zavatra tsy misy fanahy.

There is nothing without spirit.

Everything in life has meaning and purpose.

Tsy misy zaza tsy mahay mitady ny reniny.

There is no child who doesn't know how to search for their mother.

Everyone has an innate sense of connection and belonging.

Tsy misy zaza tsy mahay miteny.

There is no child who doesn't know how to

speak.

Communication and expression are inherent in human nature.

Tsy misy zaza tsy mahay mitsiky.

There is no child who doesn't know how to smile.

Joy and happiness are inherent in human nature.

Tsy misy zaza tsy manan-karena.

There is no child without wealth.

Every child has their own unique talents and abilities that make them valuable.

Tsy ny angovo no ilain'olon-dehibe, fa ny ratsy atao.

It's not the palm wine that the elders need,

but the evil done.

Wisdom comes from learning from one's mistakes.

Tsy ny hazo no voafafa, fa ny fefy.

It's not the tree that is torn, but the leaf.

Small parts often suffer the consequences of larger issues.

Tsy ny vatsy no manomboka, fa ny rano.

It's not the pot that starts, but the water.

Focus on the root causes of problems rather than treating the symptoms.

Tsy vaky volo ny tandroka.

The basket does not break hairs.

Some problems or issues are too small to

be noticed or have an impact.

Voa maro tsy mba vangiana.

Many seeds are never sown.

Not every opportunity will be taken advantage of.

Vonona hiankin'ny alika ny tompony.

Disgraced like a man whose own pet bites him.

It's shameful when someone you trust or are close to betrays you.

Zaza mitovy saina tsy mahita tsiron'omby.

A child with equal thoughts cannot see the cow's tail.

It's difficult to make progress when

everyone thinks and acts the same.

Made in the USA
Coppell, TX
17 May 2023